*C*ries *f*rom the *H*eart

Cries from the Heart

Prayers for Bereaved Parents

Margaret B. Spiess

BAKER BOOK HOUSE
Grand Rapids, Michigan 49506

Copyright 1991 by
Baker Book House Company

ISBN: 0-8010-8317-6

Printed in the United States of America

The King James Version is used for most of the Scripture quotations. Other versions used are the Revised Standard Version and the Good News Bible.

Contents

Acknowledgments   7

Why?   9
The Viewing   10
Memorial Service   11
Strength?   12
Rain   13
Shoes   14
Despair   15
Substitute   16
Shock   17
Guilt   18
A Time for Everything   19
Will He Be
   Remembered?   20
Punishment?   21
Lonely   22
Unforgiven?   23
Cast Down   24
Weary   25
The Test   26
Disconnected   27
News Report   28
Circle of Love   29
Chasm   30
Too Quiet   31
Who's in Charge?   32
How Can I Be Glad?   33
Teddy Bears   34

Compassion   35
Left Out   36
His Birthday   37
Five Minus One   38
Tears   39
Confusion   40
The Tenth
   Commandment   41
Unwilling   42
Protest   43
Frozen in Time   44
Ain't Got Time to Die   45
Polite Conversation   46
Murky Glass   47
Talk   48
Fireworks   49
Messenger   50
Let Go   51
Receptive   52
Day by Day   53
Hidden   54
For My Family   55
Reminders   56
By and By   57
The Wings of the
   Morning   58

Margaret, Marvin, and Munchkin (the family dog) riding in the side-by-side bicycle that Marvin built for his mother. The picture was taken in 1984, a few months before Marvin's death.

Acknowledgments

I am indebted to many in the writing of this book: Rev. Jim Stewart for saying, "Write your feelings down"; my husband, Erick, for his patience; and friends who are quite literally my scribes—Genny Beasley, Cathy Henry, and Sue Ann McKay.

To the memory of my son, Erick Marvin Spiess, and to those parents who have lost a child.

Why?

He's gone, Lord!
Our precious boy is gone.
Did you need another voice for your heavenly choir?
And did you need him right now?
Didn't you know he was my whole support system?
The joy of my days?
The laughter in my heart?
Why did you have to take him?
Why?
    Why?
        Why?

The Viewing

I touched his hand as he lay in his casket.
(What strange words to describe one so vital!)
All warmth and softness were gone.
There lay my son and yet not he,
this stranger, so perfect and so still.

Thank you, Lord, that this is not the end,
that "eye hath not seen,
nor ear heard,
neither have entered into the heart of man
the things which God hath prepared
for them that love him."*

*1 Corinthians 2:9

Memorial Service

With leaden feet,
   we dragged our way to church
to say our final good-byes to our son.
As we entered the sanctuary,
praise songs rang out.
Praise songs?   Now?
It was his favorite music, though,
and as it filled the air, our spirits were lifted.
It was as if he were there
showering upon us
his tenderness and caring.

It was a triumphal memorial service,
lovingly planned by his sisters and friends—
truly a celebration—
and I thank you, Lord,
from a full heart.

Strength?

They said, "Your faith is strong
and it will see you through."
Then what is this lying
shattered at my feet
like so much glass?

They said, "God only sends these
trials to those who are strong."
Then if I were weak,
would my son still be alive?

ain

We buried our son on a bright, blustery day,
but now it's raining.

He loved the warm spring rain,
but wet wintry weather
was meant for baking cookies.

Now I know, Lord, his spirit is with you.
But I loved his body, too,
his beautiful hair,
his hands I held last week.

Is it wrong, Lord,
to ask you to keep his feet warm?

Shoes

Lord, I'm going through his things,
and it's hard.
Musical instruments, keepsakes, clothes,
even the sturdy trucks
kept for the little boy
he might one day have
were not so difficult to part with.
But his shoes are not as easy.
Who could walk in his footsteps,
he who followed you so well?

I pray for the men
who get his shoes,
that they may know you, too.

Despair

Sometimes I think I can't make it
   through another day
without him.
And when I think of weeks
and months
and years
without his voice,
his laugh,
his nonsense . . .

"My tears have been my meat
day and night,
while they continually say unto me,
Where is thy God?"*

Where indeed?

*Psalm 42:3

Substitute

My wailing must surely reach heaven!
How could you take him and leave me?
Don't you know what he meant to me?
Don't you care?

While he was just beginning
    to realize his potential,
I've had a rich and rewarding life,
a happy marriage, a wonderful family,
and even the fulfillment of some of my dreams.
Parents expect to die before their children;
why didn't you take me instead of him?
I don't understand, Lord,
I don't understand.

You will have him forever;
couldn't we have kept him a little longer?

Shock

I'm grateful, Lord, for shock
that carried us through,
helping us do the unthinkable—
prepare our son for his burial.
Thank you for helping friends and family
arrange a fitting memorial
   for our beloved son.

But the shock has worn off, and
I've hit bottom with a crash.
What do I do now?

Guilt

Would he be alive now
if I had done things differently?
If I had been more assertive with the nurses?
Questioned more?
Gone to the hospital earlier?
Left later?
Prayed more?
Or differently?
The doctor was going to release him the
   next day, Lord.

I sometimes think even you were surprised
when he knocked on heaven's gate.
Did he die too soon through some
   ghastly human mistake?

A Time for Everything

How am I to accept losing him, Lord?
The weeks roll on, and it gets no easier.
He only seems farther away;
but accept I must.

"There is a . . . time to be born,
   and a time to die."*
Had he finished his work here?
Did he know something
I have yet to learn?

Help me learn my lesson well;
he paid a terrible price for it.

*Ecclesiastes 3:2

Will He Be Remembered?

He won't be forgotten,
will he, Lord?
Surely those who knew him
will now and then say,
"I knew a boy once . . ."
and tell an anecdote
which will set them all laughing.

He won't be forgotten,
will he, Lord?

Punishment?

Death is the doorway to a better life,
so why do I act as though it were a punishment
    for him
              and for us?

Help me, Lord, to stop scolding you
for taking him away.

Lonely

The days drag by, and I'm lonely, Lord,
confused about this turn my life has taken.

Hidden somewhere in this is a blessing.
Help me accept this promise:
"The eternal God is thy refuge, and underneath
    are the everlasting arms."*

*Deuteronomy 33:27

*U*nforgiven?

He died surrounded by strangers,
and we didn't even get to say good-bye.

With time, I've forgiven everyone involved
  with his passing—
everyone except myself.
When he needed me, I wasn't there,
and I can't forgive myself.

Help me, O Lord.

"For as the heaven is high above the earth,
so great is his mercy toward them that fear him.
As far as the east is from the west,
so far hath he removed our transgressions from
  us."*
Mine? Even mine?

*Psalm 103:11–12

Cast Down

"Why art thou cast down,
O my soul,
and why art thou disquieted
within me?
Hope thou in God...."*
But I did hope
and pray,
joined by all the faithful pray-ers I know.
Why did you deny my petition?
Why did you take my precious child?

*Psalm 42:5a

Weary

How weary I am of weeping, O Lord,
and jealous of those who are joyful.
Let me prove your promise:
"They that sow in tears
shall reap in joy."*
And please hasten the harvest.

*Psalm 126:5

The Test

"Every test that you have experienced
is the kind that normally comes to people.
But God keeps his promise,
and he will not allow you to be tested
beyond your power to remain firm;
at the time you are put to the test,
he will give you the strength to endure it,
and so provide you with a way out."*

Lord, I don't feel the least bit firm.
Are you sure you didn't overestimate
my capacity to endure?

*1 Corinthians 10:13 (Good News)

Disconnected

I'm cut off at the roots,
severed from all I ever believed,
sad,
confused,
disillusioned.

Time was, I felt sheltered,
secure in my faith.
Now I feel vulnerable,
exposed,
laid waste.

Don't let me shrivel and die on the vine.
Save me, Lord.

News Report

The headline reads:
"Three Members of One Family Wiped Out
   in Rollover"

Lord, I'm so ashamed!
Many are devastated,
facing bleak futures alone,
forced to live with losses
far greater than mine.

That's just it, Lord;
this is *my* loss,
and I'm having trouble coping.
The tragedies of the world move me,
but the one that hit our family
broke my heart.

Bless all those who suffer loss,
and forgive me for being selfish in my grief.

Circle of Love

When I pray for my family now,
there is a gaping hole
where his name once was.
Not to pray for him because
heaven supplies all his needs?
But what about mine?
Praying for him brings him closer.

Thank you, Lord, for the precious gift
    of my son
and for the years we had together.
Keep the circle of our love
unbroken throughout eternity.

Chasm

We're told, Lord, that you are "closer than
   breathing,
nearer than hands or feet,"*
But it's not *your* presence that I want now,
it's his.
(I'm shocked at this sacrilege,
but I must be honest.)
There seems to be a chasm
between me and my son now,
we who were so close.
Help me, Lord;
I can't deal with this.

*Tennyson, The Higher Pantheism," stanza 6

Too Quiet

Everything is too quiet, Lord.
No one revs up the car
to a steady roar.
No one plays the stereo at a volume
  to shatter glass.
No one talks to everybody who passes by,
telling his adventures.
(Even going for a loaf of bread could be a
  happening.)
And most of all,
no one sings in his deep, rich voice.
Oh, Lord, I miss him so.

Who's in Charge?

"God didn't intend your young son to die.
I'm sure of it," wrote a friend.
And in my saner moments, I agree.
But if you didn't,
who's in charge?

How Can I Be Glad?

"Rejoice evermore. . . .
In every thing give thanks;
   for this is the will of God
in Christ Jesus concerning you."*
I ought to be grateful, Lord,
but I'm finding it really hard.
I could be thankful that
      no one else was injured;
      he did not suffer long;
      he brought us great joy;
and for many other blessings you'll bring to mind.
But *rejoice?*

Help me remember your loving-kindness
and tender mercy
as I try to rejoice.

*1 Thessalonians 5:16, 18

Teddy Bears

Today we found his teddy bear,
the fur loved off
and one ear hanging by a thread,
tucked tenderly away
in a box at the back of his closet.

When young children, some newly minted,
are recalled by their maker,
away from the coziness of home,
does heaven bewilder them?
Where are the teddy bears?
Are there puppies and kittens?
Will an angel sing them to sleep?

Comfort, dear Lord,
   those who have lost little ones,
and hold them in the hollow of your hand.

Compassion

"Blessed are they that mourn:
for they shall be comforted."*
Remind me, Lord,
I'm not the only mourner,
and people grieve in many ways;
some seek solace in drugs or alcohol,
others retire from life,
and some leave their beloved's room untouched.
Let me show compassion
to those whose ways seem strange to me,
and comfort all who are heavyhearted today.

*Matthew 5:4

Left Out

Have I neglected my husband
and my daughters
while focusing on my own distress?
You and I know the answer to that!
Forgive me as I try to make things right,
and, O Lord, help them to forgive me, too.

His Birthday

Today is his birthday, Lord,
and I should be scurrying about
planning surprises.
But he's blowing out celestial candles
and being serenaded by the heavenly choir.

If I had known his time would be so short,
would I have done things differently?
Listened better?
Shown more patience?
Celebrated often?
I hope so.
Oh, I hope so.

Five Minus One

We are four,
who once were five,
and the change bewilders us.

We were catapulted onstage
by the divine director,
                                  unprepared,
to take—as if we could—
   the roles *he* filled with ease and grace.

Who will be his dad's best friend?
Who will love his sisters as he did?
And oh, dear Lord,
   who will laugh and sing with me?

*T*ears

"The tears . . . streamed down,
and I let them flow as freely as they would,
making of them a pillow for my heart.
On them it rested."*

Thank you, Lord, for the healing gift of tears.

*Augustine, "Confessions" IX:12

Confusion

"The LORD hath appeared of old
unto me, saying, Yea, I have loved
thee with an everlasting love:
therefore with lovingkindness have
I drawn thee."*

That's a strange way to show love,
taking him away from this life
he enjoyed so much.
But wait—I'm forgetting
that it's heaven you drew him to.
    I get confused, Lord.

*Jeremiah 31:3

The Tenth Comandment

"Thou shalt not covet . . . anything that is thy
   neighbor's."*
But I do, Lord, I do!
I covet the sons of others.
I wonder why they are living when my boy is not.

It's ridiculous.
Could I be losing my mind?
Forgive me, Lord, for being jealous.
I really don't want to wish misfortune on anyone.

*Exodus 20:17

*U*nwilling

I awakened with a heavy heart today, Lord, unwilling to face another day without him.

But "this is the day which the LORD hath made"; help me "rejoice and be glad in it."*

*Psalm 118:24

Protest

We're moving cross country tomorrow
according to previous plans,
and I can't, Lord. I really can't!
It's asking too much
to move away from all reminders of him
and not to have anyone
who knew him
to talk with.

It's too much.
It's just too much!

Frozen in Time

As I dusted his picture this morning,
I noticed how unchanged he is,
while we grow older every day.
It's as if he's frozen in time,
forever young.
Or is he changing, too,
in ways we cannot know?

How will we ever recognize each other
when we meet again?

Ain't Got Time to Die

"Oh, I keep so busy working for my Master.
Keep so busy working for my Master.
Keep so busy working for my Master.
Ain't got time to die."
This was his favorite spiritual.
But he did die,
when he was desperately needed here.

What can he be doing there
that's so important, Lord?

Polite Conversation

"How many children do you have?"

If I answer correctly,
I deny him, and he is lost again.

Show me how to make polite conversation
when my heart is breaking.

Murky Glass

Only the good die young, they say,
while many ill and elderly
beg to go.
Often it seems
those who are needed most
are taken early.

I sometimes view death through a murky glass.
Clear my vision, Lord.

Talk

If only we could talk together
about his death,
airing our feelings,
without limitations—
no one saying, "Don't feel that way,"
or "Don't cry, Momma."
But we're afraid to hurt too much.

Lord, dissolve our guilt and anger.
Shine on our dark and heavy places
and heal our wounds.

Fireworks

He saw his first fireworks from a car bed,
and the noise frightened him.
Afterward, the Fourth of July
became his favorite celebration.
Now I can hardly watch fireworks without crying.

But that is not right.
Those were some of the happiest times
   for our family.
He wouldn't want me to be sad.

Help me get my reactions in order, Lord,
and to remember with joy
all the warm and wonderful times
we had together.

Messenger

Once, while I was sleeping,
I heard him call my name.
My eyes flew open,
but he was gone.

Lord, I thank you for love
that transcends even the barrier of death.
Send him often as your messenger.
I miss him so!

Let Go

There's nothing I can do to bring him back,
but by keeping my stubborn grip on grief
I may be preventing his progress
in his new home.

Help me let go, Lord,
and obtain the joy and gladness promised
   in your Word.*

*Isaiah 35:10

Receptive

Lord, help me be receptive
to the blessings you have prepared for me.
I spend much time bewailing my fate,
holding my hand out, begging,
not stopping long enough to accept.

Thank you for comforting me all this time,
and open my eyes to your daily gifts.

Day by Day

Lord, I need strength
not only for the long haul
but for each minute as it passes.
Let me begin each day
with praise
and end it with thanksgiving.
Cleanse my mind of gloomy thoughts
and fill me with gladness and hope.

Hidden

My thoughts whirl, like leaves in a storm,
with a thousand questions
about suffering and death.
I search in vain for the answers,
but I'll know on the other side.
"For nothing is hid that shall not be made
manifest, nor anything secret that shall
not be known and come to light."*

*Luke 8:17 (RSV)

For My Family

Surely, Lord, they know
if one of them had died instead,
I would have been just as devastated.

Have you told them?

Reminders

I miss the things we shared—
romping with the dog,
building a snowman,
baking cookies,
splashing in the lake—
but now and then my heart is pierced
by a keen sense of loss
when I haven't even been thinking of him.

Bless those whose grief is new,
and bless me as I try to cope.

By and By

Lord, it's the anniversary of his death,
and maybe someday I'll be ready to celebrate,
knowing he's safe with you.
There will always be a hole in my heart,
but I thank you from the depths of my being
for his irrepressible spirit
and his whimsical view of life.
Thank you for lending him to us,
however brief the while,
and grant that we may soar together by and by.

The Wings of the Morning

"Whither shall I go from thy spirit?
or whither shall I flee from thy presence?
    If I ascend up into heaven,
        thou art there:
    if I make my bed in hell,
        behold, thou art there.
If I take the wings of the morning,
and dwell in the uttermost parts of the sea;
Even there shall thy hand lead me,
and thy right hand shall hold me.
If I say, Surely the darkness shall cover me;
even the night shall be light about me.
Yea, the darkness hideth not from thee;
but the night shineth as the day:
the darkness and the light are both alike
    to thee."*

Help me, Lord,
to claim this precious promise
for him and for us
today.

*Psalm 139:7–12